Getting to Know Children and Their Families

A Framework of Questions to Help Social Workers Gather Appropriate Information

Asmita Parmar
and
Pat Spatcher

Russell House Publishing

First published in 2005 by:
Russell House Publishing Ltd.
4 St George's House
Uplyme Road
Lyme Regis
Dorset DT7 3LS

Tel: 01297-443948
Fax: 01297-442722
e-mail: help@russellhouse.co.uk
www.russellhouse.co.uk

British Library Cataloguing-in-publication Data:
A catalogue record for this book is available from the British Library.

ISBN: 1-903855-77-2; 9781-903855-77-5

Typeset by TW Typesetting, Plymouth, Devon

Printed by Cromwell Press Ltd, Trowbridge, Wiltshire

Russell House Publishing

Is a group of social work, probation, education and youth and community work practitioners and academics working in collaboration with a professional publishing team.
Our aim is to work closely with the field to produce innovative and valuable materials to help managers, trainers, practitioners and students.
We are keen to receive feedback on publications and new ideas for future projects.

This feedback was given to the authors when this book was being field-tested . . .

I have found this useful when looking at life-story work with a child aged eight years old when exploring his family and social networks. Also what he liked to do, which helped me plan the work I would be doing with him.

(A student social worker on placement in a primary school setting in inner London)

I would find this so useful when visiting families as I cannot remember all the concepts of the triangle and when I get back to the office I find that I have missed out pieces of relevant and vital information to inform my assessment. If I had a copy of this book with me, I could pick out the relevant questions that I need information for so that this would save me time in needing to contact the family again for more information before a service is provided from social services.

(A social worker in an initial assessment team in a deprived London borough)

I think this book would be a useful tool for the social workers in my team to use as a guide to asking questions relevant to initial assessments to offer effective support to children and their families.

(A manager of an initial assessment team in Hertfordshire)

This would be a good learning tool not only for social workers but would recommend it for student social workers when on placements in children and families settings both in field teams and in the voluntary sector.

(A lecturer teaching law in a London university)

When I am carrying outreach assessments of young people discharged from the unit this would inform me linking in with the assessment framework and the questions and sharing my social work values with the mental health professionals within my team.

(A social worker within a multi-disciplinary team
(child and adolescent mental health team) in Hertfordshire)

This feedback was given to the authors when this book was being field-tested . . .

I was able to use this when linking in and making a formal assessment and asking questions of the parent and two sisters who had been abused by their step-father allegedly while involved in s.47 of the Children Act 1989.

(A social work student on placement in a secondary school
in a deprived London borough)

This is extremely useful for any newly qualified social workers who hesitate when visiting families and have anxiety around gathering essential information to inform how social services can support the family.

(Consultant from a social work agency)

This book would not be useful for cases of unaccompanied minors as it does not fit with our assessment process but if the unaccompanied minor was to have a baby then we would find this very useful in looking at the holistic needs of mother providing baby's needs within the community.

(A manager in an unaccompanied minors asylum team in London)

Contents

Acknowledgements

We would like to thank our husbands for their patience and support while we were compiling the book.

We should also like to thank all the colleagues and professionals we approached in our research.

Our special thanks to Trish for her support and guidance in our endeavours.

About the Authors

Asmita has spent several years in a Social Work Statutory Children and Families team. She has a BA in Social Work and a Diploma in counselling.

Pat has spent nearly forty years in social work practice, both in statutory and voluntary work, mainly in the children and families field. She is currently working independently as a freelance practitioner in a variety of roles.

Introduction

For practitioners and students this is an easy-to-use tool for use when undertaking any kind of children and families social work, and in particular the initial and comprehensive assessments with families based on the *Framework for Assessment* (DoH, 2000).

It is a reminder of 'what to think about' to make sure that appropriate information is gathered for a holistic view of a child's needs and how carers are meeting them. Its helpful design provides:

◆ Suggestions and prompts to the information that often must be gathered when making family visits under tight time constraints.

◆ A photocopiable framework in which to record the information.

◆ Selections of useful questions that are appropriate to children of different ages.

The Framework for Assessment

The *Framework for Assessment* introduced by the Department of Health was the result of many enquiries that have taken place over the last decade (Reder, Duncan and Gray, 2002). *Messages from Research* (DoH, 1995) highlighted the difficulties practitioners faced during assessment. The framework provides a structure for assessing not only the child's development needs but also the parents' capacity to meet those needs and the environment in which the child lives.

Experiences of working with the Framework for Assessment

Before the introduction of the DoH's *Framework for Assessment* agencies involved in children and families work had their own assessment frameworks that they worked with. This caused duplication, fragmented interagency working, and families repeating their needs to the various professionals they were involved with. With the implementation of the *Framework for Assessment* the intention was for all agencies to work in the same way, thus avoiding the need to have more than one interview and the risk of different sets of information. This depends solely on agencies having a multi agency approach to the families they are working with. Although this has evolved primarily as a social work tool, other agencies' contributions are essential to ensure that an accurate and informed assessment is undertaken.

From our own experiences as social work practitioners, using the Framework, and talking with colleagues both within children and families social work and within health, it has come to our attention that some practitioners were nevertheless questioning aspects of their involvement with families. For example, when carrying out an initial or core assessment, were they gathering the appropriate information, or just gathering information with no meaning? This problem evolved from the fact that the framework is a recording rather than an assessment tool and as such requires professionals to generate the appropriate questions according to each presenting case. It was for this reason we explored the usefulness of an extra tool to support practitioners during the process of assessment by articulating questions which could support their assessment practice.

About this book

When doing the assessment various questions have to be asked, and the exemplar forms completed. We have looked at the initial and comprehensive framework forms in detail and have devised a set of questions as a guideline for social workers and other practitioners to refer to or use when engaging with a family and deciding what assessment information is required.

Many people who have used the questions during their development and testing have told us that the questions are of use. A sample of their comments is printed at the front of this book. But it is important to keep in mind that each practitioner may think of others besides these, which they can add on to support their own way of working.

When compiling and testing these questions based on the Framework our goal was that they should be a useful tool for student social workers and qualified social workers, both those who are already working with children and families, and those who may be thinking about doing so when their studies have been completed.

The framework of questions in this book

Within the questions we have obviously used the criteria as laid out in the *Framework for Assessment* (DoH, 2000). See Figure 1.

> *The framework in this guidance is developed from the legislative foundations and principles in Chapter 1 and an extensive research and practice knowledge which is outlined in the practice guidance (DoH, 2000a). It requires a thorough understanding of:*
>
> ◆ *the developmental needs of children;*
>
> ◆ *the capacities of parents or caregivers to respond appropriately to those needs;*
>
> ◆ *the impact of wider family and environmental factors on parenting capacity and children.*
>
> (DoH, 2000a: 17)

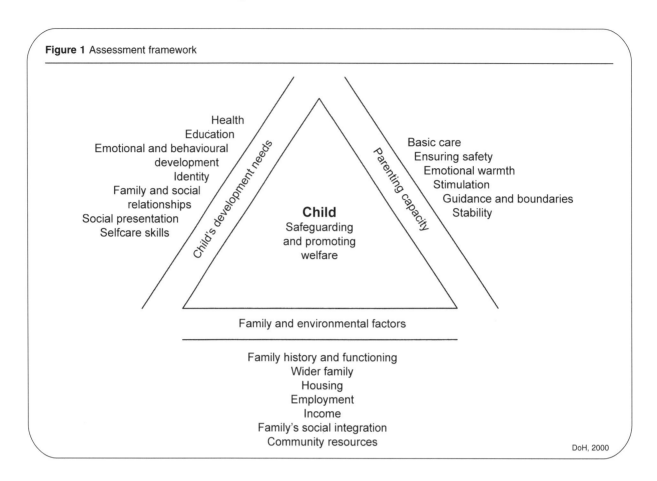

Figure 1 Assessment framework

A summary of these principles is provided in the next section of this book.

To help you gather evidence concerning the developmental needs of babies, children and young people the subsequent sections of this book contain lists of questions to put to the parents or carers that are appropriate to five different age groups:

◆ Babies up to 24 months old

◆ 2, 3 and 4 year old children

◆ Children between aged 5 and 9 years old

◆ Children between aged 10 and 14 years old

◆ Children over the age of 15

It may be that some of the questions can only be answered by the child's parent or carer but wherever appropriate and possible the child should be involved in answering the questions and expressing their wishes and preferences.

The Framework for Assessment

This section of the book conveniently summarises the underlying principles of the *Framework for Assessment* that can be found on pages 10–16 of the DOH's document (DoH, 2000a) that can be read and downloaded from the DfES website on www.dfes.gov.uk

 ◆ It is summarised here so that it can easily be carried with you when visiting families.

 ◆ Anyone who is familiar with this material can perhaps skip this section but may find useful the rationale it provides, for using the framework of questions that follows in this book.

 ◆ Anyone who seeks a broader and critical treatment of the issues raised can be recommended to read Martin C. Calder's extensively referenced critique and reformulation of the assessment framework on pages 3–61 in Calder and Hackett (2003) and Calder (2000) for child sexual abuse (pages 5–8 are particularly relevant).

Underpinning principles

The *Framework for Assessment* is underpinned by principles that are the focus of work with children and families.

Assessments:

 ◆ *are child centred;*

 ◆ *are rooted in child development;*

 ◆ *are ecological in their approach;*

 ◆ *ensure equality of opportunity;*

 ◆ *involve working with children and families;*

 ◆ *build on strengths as well as identify difficulties;*

 ◆ *are inter-agency in their approach to assessment and the provision of services;*

 ◆ *are a continuing process, not a single event;*

 ◆ *are carried out in parallel with other action and providing services;*

 ◆ *are grounded in evidence based knowledge.*

(DoH, 2000: 10)

From the framework, and enlarging on the above to emphasise what the assessment process is all about when working with families in need, it is very important to look at upbringing in its widest context as the histories of families has a bearing on present relationships and cultural issues to inform the assessment.

It is very important to look at all the information gathered during an assessment and then form an opinion based on that evidence before coming to a conclusion. This will inform what help and support is needed for the family, which will inform the care, child protection and family support plan.

Looking at the principles in more detail and highlighting the main areas of the assessment process as outlined in the *Framework for Assessment* one gets the view and opinion that the Department of Health was very clear about how to focus the work. Social workers and other professionals involved in the initial and comprehensive assessment with families should follow the guidelines and recommendations.

The Department of Health highlights the importance of working in a child centred way. The following is useful to consider in conjunction with the questions to follow when assessing children and their families:

Child centred

According to the Children Act 1989 (White et al., 1991) the Welfare Checklist Section 1.1.–1.3. quotes:

(a) the ascertainable wishes and feelings of the child concerned (considered in the light of his age and understanding);

(b) his physical, emotional and educational needs;

(c) the likely effect on him of any change in his circumstances;

(d) his age, sex, background and any characteristic of his which the court considers relevant;

(e) any harm which he has suffered or is at risk of suffering;

(f) how capable each of his parents, and any other person in relation to whom the court considers the matter relevant, is of meeting his needs;

(g) the range of powers available to the court under this Act in the proceedings in question.

This takes into account the child's perspective throughout this process depending on age and understanding.

> *The importance, therefore, of undertaking direct work with children during assessment is emphasised, including developing multiple, age, gender and culturally appropriate methods for ascertaining their wishes and feelings, and understanding the meaning of their experiences to them. Throughout the assessment process, the safety of the child should be ensured.*
>
> (DoH, 2000: 10)

Rooted in child development

It is important that the social worker and other professionals have a thorough understanding of child development to work with children and their families.

Children have a range of different and complex developmental needs which must be met during different stages of childhood if optimal outcomes are to be achieved.

(DoH, 2000: 11)

If outcomes are to be achieved once an assessment has been completed, whether initial or core assessment, it needs to be rooted in child development.

Children with special needs may have different rates of development depending on their particular circumstances and reach their milestones at very different stages than a child without special needs.

For example, in the early years there is an emphasis on developing cognitive and language skills, achieving physical milestones and forming secure attachments; in middle childhood, social and educational development becomes more prominent; while the adolescent strives to reconcile the tensions between social and emotional dependence and independence.

(DoH, 2000: 11)

Each child's development depends on the family circumstances, particular experiences they have been exposed to, their individual ability to understand what is going on around them, their own individual special need for support and help, cultural implications and where they are living. The list is endless.

Families who have a child in need of services from social workers and other professionals for a variety of reasons are often vulnerable, isolated due to cultural, language difficulties etc., and the children are not receiving help and support. It is important that social workers and other professionals have a good understanding of child development and what they are hoping to achieve when working in partnership with families:

Plans and interventions should be based on a clear assessment of the developmental progress and difficulties a child may be experiencing and ensure that planned action is timely and appropriate in terms of the child's developmental needs.

(DoH, 2000: 11)

Workers need to ensure that the focus of their assessment addresses cognitive/emotional as well as physical development, and also addresses adolescent development, since the framework provides guidance ostensibly for under eights.

Ecological in their approach

The significance of understanding the parent-child relationship has long been part of child welfare practice: less so the importance of the interface between environmental factors and a child's development, and the influence of these environmental factors on parents' capacities to respond to their child's needs.

(Jack, 1997; Stevenson, 1998 and others in DoH, 2000: 11)

So in other words when doing an assessment with families it is not only important to look at the child's developmental needs but also the parents' abilities to meet those basic needs (parenting capacity). The environmental factors i.e. extended family, friends, networks and the area in which the family live, work, housing, finance, go to school, play etc., has an impact on the parenting of some children. By taking account of all the above a fuller more comprehensive assessment and outcomes can be formulated when working with families.

Assessment, therefore, should take account of three domains:

- ◆ *the child's developmental needs;*

- ◆ *the parents' or caregivers' capacities to respond appropriately;*

- ◆ *the wider family and environmental factors.*

(DoH, 2000: 12)

The DfES has developed the Home Inventory in the last few years to support the assessment procedure by providing detailed guidance in the assessment of parent-child interactions.

Ensure equality of opportunity

The Children Act 1989 is built on the premise that 'children and young people and their parents should all be considered as individuals with particular needs and potentialities' (DoH, 1989), that differences in bringing up children due to family structures, religion, culture and ethnic origins should be respected and understood and that those children with 'specific social needs arising out of disability or health condition' have their assessed needs met and reviewed (DoH, 1998a).

(DoH, 2000: 12)

By working this way a family's needs within the assessment process are taken into account.

Involve working with children and families

It is important when working with individual families that the child's needs are central to the work that is trying to be achieved within the assessment. It is important to listen and engage with all members of the family (if appropriate),and to focus not only on the immediate concerns and issues, but to look at the wider picture. For example, what help do the family need and what are they asking for; or are there more pressing problems around child protection (which in itself is another issue).

It is important to develop a working relationship with children and members of their family in order to make a full assessment of the problems and reach outcomes in partnership with the family as a whole, and this may be more difficult when complying with the strict timescales for assessment.

Parents value taking part in deciding on what help they need, they will respond more favourably if they are part of the discussions and decisions are not made without consulting them throughout the process. This is particularly important when trying to engage with children and young people. They will listen and take part in discussions more if they feel they are being 'listened to', and taken note of. Decisions made in partnership have a better outcome when all parties are engaged in the process.

In the case of child protection, or a child with special needs, it is important to remember that this is a different set of problems. Professionals involved have to take the lead in most cases because of the situation a child may find themselves in: they need protecting as the parent or adults in their lives are unable to do this for one reason or another. However:

> *Studies have found that even in situations where child sexual abuse is alleged, despite early difficulties that may arise because of having to take immediate child protective action, it may still be possible to work with children and their parents* (Cleaver and Freeman, 1995; Jones and Ramchandani, 1999).
>
> (DoH, 2000: 13)

Build on strengths as well as identify difficulties

> *It is important that an approach to assessment, which is based on a full understanding of what is happening to a child in the context of his or her family and the wider community, examines carefully the nature of the interactions between the child, family and the environmental factors and identifies both positive and negative influences.*
>
> (DoH, 2000: 13)

Obviously these will differ depending on the child and their circumstances, the problems, obstacles, and the difficulties that are identified from talking and engaging with the child, family and friends if necessary.

It is important not only to look at the positive aspects of the care the parent or carer is giving to their family, but to look at the negative issues that cause problems within the home and in the wider community. In some cases this affects the way the parents can support their children and young people as they are growing up. Again, it is important to look at the whole picture and not just the family in isolation.

The crisis could be over health, financial or housing issues. The children could not be attending school for various reasons; the family may be isolated due to language and cultural difficulties. The child of the family may have special needs and the parent is isolated because of this. Once the assessment process identifies and highlights the support the family needs they can be put in touch with supporting agencies in the community.

Inter-agency in their approach to assessment and the provision of services

When a child is born, irrespective whether they are from 'families in need' or not, they will become involved with a variety of different professionals i.e. health agencies, and schools. From the work the professionals do, they will identify children who are vulnerable as needing help and support and this is where social services come in. The knowledge that these professionals from different agencies have about the family is extremely important and that is why they are part of the assessment process. This enables the social worker to gain a fuller picture of the family in order to work with them.

> *An important underlying principle of the approach to assessment in this Guidance, therefore, is that it is based on a inter-agency model in which it is not just social services departments which are the assessors and providers of services.*
>
> (DoH, 2000: 14)

This illustrates that it is vital that all professionals, not only social workers, have a responsibility to complete their part in the initial and core assessments to achieve the best outcome for the child.

A continuing process, not a single event

> *Understanding what is happening to a vulnerable child within the context of his or her family and the local community cannot be achieved as a single event.*
>
> (DoH, 2000: 14)

It is important when doing an initial assessment with a family that you are aware of the referral beforehand, whether they are known to social services, what input other agencies may have had with the family in the past or now.

It is very important when gathering the evidence for the initial assessment from parents, carers, engaging with their children or young people etc., that you look at all aspects of the family. When forming a conclusion i.e. plan of action, with the family, it is important to focus on the evidence gathering and form a plan of action once all the information has been gathered.

This assessment process involves one or more of the following:

◆ *establishing good working relationships with the child and the family;*

◆ *developing a deeper understanding through multiple approaches to the assessment task;*

◆ *setting up joint or parallel assessment arrangements with other professionals and agencies, as appropriate;*

◆ *determining which types of intervention are most likely to be effective for which needs.*

> (DoH, 2000: 14)

For many families who have contact with social services for one reason or another, this could be a 'one off situation', where the family get help for a particular problem and never need help and support again. However in many cases social services and other agencies work with families on a number of occasions, often supporting them over a period of years for one reason or another. When engaging with social services and other agencies the family concerned is assessed, their individual needs are looked at and plans formulated. In these situations and where the child's safety is not in doubt the work takes place together or the family are referred on to other agencies for support.

In situations where a child is at risk for one reason or another, questions will have to be looked at with the parents and what help and support they need. In the case of children with special needs looking at the impact on the services the family may or may not be having, as well as the implications for the family in caring for a child with a disability.

Child protection is a very different situation, where social services (supported by other agencies) take the lead, and try and look at the problems that have been identified or the abuse that has taken place. Still in this situation it is important to remember to engage with the family, and look at the whole picture from the point of view of the child or young person concerned and the wider picture as it presents itself.

The assessment should continue throughout the period of involvement from social services and the other agencies working in partnership as far as possible with the family members depending on the circumstances of the referral.

> *In order to achieve the best outcomes, the framework should be used also at important decision making times when reviewing the child's progress and future plans.*
>
> (DoH, 2000: 15)

Carried out in parallel with other action and providing services

> *Undertaking an assessment with a family can begin a process of understanding and change by key family members. A practitioner may, during the process of gathering information, be instrumental in bringing about change by the questions asked, by listening to members of the family, by validating the family's difficulties or concerns, and by providing information and advice.*
>
> (DoH, 2000: 15)

If possible, when doing an assessment with a family, work can be started before the full assessment is completed i.e. referral to a clinic or counsellor for support then it would be good practice to try and get this underway. It may be possible to set up meetings and appointments for the family with regards to education for their children etc. It is important for referrals or appointments to be set up early, then the intervention and support the family need may be better received, and a crisis may be avoided in the future.

Grounded in evidence based knowledge

Within the *Framework for Assessment* the DoH (2000) looks at the importance of basing the work on a particular theoretical base, related to research from the point of view of all the professionals involved in the process, with its many different disciplines from the point of view of the medical and social model.

> *Practice is also based on policies laid down in legislation and government guidance. It is essential that practitioners and their managers ensure that practice and its supervision are grounded in the most up to date knowledge and that they make use of the resources described in the practice guidance as well as other critical materials including:*
>
> ◈ *relevant research findings;*
>
> ◈ *national and local statistical data;*
>
> ◈ *national policy and practice guidance;*
>
> ◈ *Social Services Inspectorate Inspection Standards;*

◆ *Government and local inspection, audit and performance assessment reports;*

◆ *lessons learnt from national and local enquiries and reviews of cases of child maltreatment.*

(DoH, 2000: 16)

Not only does the framework look at the theoretical base, but it expects the practice of the professionals working with the family to be evidence based. The framework guidance looks at the whole approach to the assessment to be undertaken as follows:

◆ *use knowledge critically from research and practice about the needs of children and families and the outcomes of services and interventions to inform their assessment and planning;*

◆ *record and update information systematically, distinguishing sources of information for example direct observation, other agency record or interviews with family members;*

◆ *learn from the views of users of services i.e., children and families;*

◆ *valuate continuously whether the intervention is effective in responding to the needs of an individual child and family and modifying their interventions accordingly;*

◆ *evaluate rigorously the information, processes and outcomes from the practitioner's own interventions to develop practice wisdom.*

(DoH, 2000: 16)

When doing the assessment various questions have to be asked, and the forms completed. We have looked at the initial and comprehensive framework forms in detail and have devised a set of questions as a guideline for social workers to refer to or use when engaging with a family. We hope that the questions are of use, but obviously there are many more that the individual practitioner may think of besides these, which they can add to for their own way of working.

We felt when compiling these questions based on the framework that they would be a useful tool for student social workers and social workers alike working in the field of children and families or those thinking about doing so when their studies have been completed.

Questions about Babies up to 24 Months Old

The Baby's Developmental Needs

Health

1. Does your baby have any illness or disability such as:
 	
   ◆ diabetes
 	
   ◆ asthma
 	
   ◆ epilepsy
 	
   ◆ food allergies
 	
   ◆ other special needs	

2. Are you giving your baby any medication?	
3. Did you have a normal delivery? Did you have problems having your baby?	
4. Is your baby feeding well?	
5. Are you registered with a GP? Are your baby's health checks and injections up to date? *Obtain details and permission for assessment and agency checks.*	

Getting to Know Children and Their Families, Parmar and Spatcher (2005) Russell House Publishing

6. Do you have a health visitor? How often do you see your health visitor?	
7. Does your baby sleep well?	
8. Do you have any problems concerning your baby's health?	
9. Does your baby like their food?	
10. Does your baby still wear a nappy?	

Education

11. Does your baby recognise you when you talk and play with them?	
12. How does your baby respond to: ◆ you ◆ their brothers and sisters ◆ other family members and strangers?	
13. Does your baby have any toys to play with?	

Emotional and Behavioural Development

14. Is your baby:
    ◆ sitting
    ◆ crawling
    ◆ starting to take their first steps?	

15. Is your baby happy and content?	
16. Does your baby have problems, e.g. are they clingy or have they any other problem? *It is important to find out about sleep patterns particularly with a new baby, and how the parents are coping.*	
17. Do you have any person to help you with your baby? If so how does baby get on with them?	
18. When your baby cries how do you respond?	
19. Who does your baby get on with in the family?	
20. How does your baby settle at night and wake up in the morning? *Look at the family routines i.e. mealtimes, food and where and when they sleep.*	

Getting to Know Children and Their Families, Parmar and Spatcher (2005) Russell House Publishing

21. Is your baby talking and responding to you, when you talk and play with them? If not has your baby got:
 	
   ◆ special needs
 	
   ◆ hearing difficulties
 	
   ◆ sight problems
 	
   ◆ learning disabilities
 	
   ◆ other illness?
 	
Professionals need to think about the importance of the health visitor being involved at this stage in the baby's developmental needs.	

Identity

22. Does your baby know their own name and respond to their name?	
23. Do you take your baby with you to family gatherings?	
24. In which country was your baby born? *Look at ethnic origin and culture.*	
25. Who does your baby get on well with, within the family, friends etc.?	

Family and Social Relationships

26. Do you look after your baby at home, or does someone else:
 	
    ◆ at a nursery
 	
    ◆ in your extended family
 	
    ◆ a child minder	

27. If you have a partner which one of you takes care of your baby's needs?	
28. Who is your baby more attached to?	
29. How do your other children get on with your baby?	
30. Do you attend a mother and baby group?	

31. Do you take your baby:
 	
    ◆ swimming
 	
    ◆ shopping
 	
    ◆ to meet other parents
 	
    ◆ to any other activities?
 	
Is this as a family event?	

Getting to Know Children and Their Families, Parmar and Spatcher (2005) Russell House Publishing

32. Do you have any pets?
     If so how is your baby protected from
     them?	

Social Presentation

Observe whether the baby is well cared for i.e. is it clean (no smells) well clothed and without any visible bruises. There could be 'family in need' or child protection issues.

Parenting Capacity

Basic Care

33. Is your baby: ◆ feeding well ◆ sleeping well ◆ having teething problems?	
34. Where is the baby sleeping? ◆ Is the room well aired and warm? ◆ Is the bedding clean? ◆ Are any other children sharing the room?	
35. What milk are you feeding your baby?	
36. Do you always keep your appointments with the health visitor and GP?	
37. If your baby has any medical conditions, special needs or are on medication, how does this affect your care for them?	

Ensuring Safety

38. Is there adequate safety: ◆ in the kitchen ◆ on the stairs ◆ access to the front and back doors and the garden?	

Getting to Know Children and Their Families, Parmar and Spatcher (2005) Russell House Publishing

39. Are there safeguards to prevent accidents?	
40. Has your baby had any injuries? Was there an explanation? (accidental). If yes what happened, how was it dealt with? What is the situation now?	
41. Is the baby left with other adults apart from parents or carers? ◆ extended family ◆ neighbours ◆ friends	

Emotional Warmth

Observe the interaction of the parents with the baby, e.g. is the baby distressed and clinging or happy and content in the presence of parents?

42. How do you comfort your baby when they are upset or crying?	
43. Do you talk to your baby? How (praise or rejection)?	

Stimulation

Observe the parent or carer playing and encouraging their baby in play. If the baby has special needs observe how the parent or carer stimulates play and exercise.

44. Are there adequate toys for your baby to play with in a safe environment?	

45. Do you take your baby out? Where?	
46. Does your baby play with your other children?	
47. Do you attend 'sure start', a mother and baby group or a nursery?	

Guidance and Boundaries

48. What is your baby's routine? ◆ sleeping ◆ feeding ◆ playing ◆ bathing	
49. Are you working? If so who looks after your baby? For how long?	
50. If your child is looked after by a childminder, are they registered?	

Stability

51. Have you always cared for your child? If not, why not? (one for all).	

52. Do you have contact with family members or significant others? If not, why not?	
53. How would you describe your relationship with your child? *Explore with the parents the consistency of the close bond between them and their child.*	

Issues Affecting Parents or Carers

54. Do you have physical disabilities or mental health needs? If yes, how does this affect the care of your children?	
55. Have you had contact with social services before as an adult or a child or with your own children? If yes, when, how and why?	
56. Have you been in a relationship involving domestic violence in the past? Are you now?	
57. Have you had a problem with drink or substance misuse in the past? Do you still?	

Family and Environmental Factors

Family History

58. What is your ethnic origin? What is your partner's ethnic origin?	
59. What was your childhood like?	
60. Did you live: ◆ with your parents ◆ in an extended family ◆ in care ◆ in this country ◆ abroad	
61. Is English your first language? If not, what is it?	
62. Do both the adults and the children in your family speak English?	

Family Functioning

63. Apart from you and your children who else lives in the house? How are they related to you and your children?	

Getting to Know Children and Their Families, Parmar and Spatcher (2005) Russell House Publishing

64. Have there been any changes in the household recently, such as: ◆ a parent leaving ◆ an older child leaving home ◆ members of your extended family coming to stay ◆ a child going to live with your extended family?	
65. How do your children get on together? Do some of them get on better together than others? If so, why?	
66. If you do not live with your child's birth parent, how do you get on with them?	
67. How much contact do they have with the children? *If the birth parent that does not live in the household is different for different children, ask about each one.*	
68. If your child has special needs, what impact does this have on you and your other children?	
69. How do you handle rows, disputes, and differences of opinion in the care of your children with your partner or extended family?	

Wider Family

70. Who from your extended family supports you with:
 	
  ◆ practical help
 	
  ◆ emotional support
 	
  ◆ financial support
 	
  ◆ interpreting
 	
  ◆ special needs help?	

Housing

71. Where do you live:
 	
  ◆ In a council house
 	
  ◆ In your own property
 	
  ◆ In B&B accommodation?	

72. How many bedrooms are there?	
73. Have all the children a bed of their own? If not, why not?	
74. Are there sufficient heating, lighting, cooking, toilet and bath facilities for the family? If not, why not?	
75. Is the home overcrowded? *Observe the hygiene, cleanliness and basic care adults are giving to the children for their emotional, and physical well-being.*	

Getting to Know Children and Their Families, Parmar and Spatcher (2005) Russell House Publishing

Employment and Income

76. Are you or your partner working? If not, why not?	

77. What benefits do you receive?
 	
   ◆ child benefit
 	
   ◆ housing benefit
 	
   ◆ (is the child support agency involved)
 	
   ◆ job seekers allowance
 	
   ◆ income support
 	
   ◆ disability living allowance
 	
   ◆ family tax credit.	

78. Do you receive money from an ex-husband or ex-partner?	
79. If you are working, are you aware of the financial support you can get?	
80. Are you managing on the money or are you in debt? *If they are not managing, suggest that they contact their local citizens advice bureau.*	

81. Do you budget for your bills:
 	
   ◆ gas and electricity
 	
   ◆ rent
 	
   ◆ council tax
 	
   ◆ TV licence
 	
   ◆ food and school dinners
 	
   ◆ clothes
 	
   ◆ debts, loans
 	
   ◆ bus fares?	

Family Social Integration

82. Do you have friends in the area? If not, do you feel isolated? Is this due to language and cultural problems?	
83. Do you practice a religion? Do you attend a mosque, a temple, a church etc.?	
84. Do you feel or experience discrimination or harassment in the community in which you live?	

Community Resources

85. Do you travel by public transport to access these? If so how far is it from your home?	

Getting to Know Children and Their Families, Parmar and Spatcher (2005) Russell House Publishing

86. How easy is it for you to take your family on a bus or train? *This would depend on whether they have other small children as well, or a child with special needs.*	
87. Do you use the local community resources in the area: ◆ shops and supermarket ◆ library ◆ leisure activities ◆ GP/health visitor/school nurse ◆ school?	
88. Are all the family needs for leisure activities met in your local area? (Including special needs provision and children and young people's clubs). Is transport provided for them?	

Questions for 2, 3 and 4 Year Old Children

The Child's Developmental Needs

Health

1. Does your child have any illness or disability such as: ◆ diabetes ◆ asthma ◆ epilepsy ◆ food allergies ◆ other special needs	
2. Are you giving your child any medication?	
3. Did you have a normal delivery? Did you have problems having your baby?	
4. Is your child feeding well?	
5. Are you registered with a GP? Are your child's health checks and injections up to date? *Obtain details and permission for assessment and agency checks.*	

Getting to Know Children and Their Families, Parmar and Spatcher (2005) Russell House Publishing

6. Do you have a health visitor? How often do you see your health visitor?	
7. Does your child sleep well?	
8. Do you have any problems concerning your child's health?	
9. Does your child like their food?	
10. Does your child still wear a nappy?	

Education/Day Care

11. Does your child go to a nursery school or pre-school? If so, how do they get on there?	
12. Do you read to or play with your child?	
13. Does your child like playing with their toys? Which are their favourites and why?	

14. Is your child able to tell you what they want if they are: ◆ hungry; ◆ wanting to use the toilet; ◆ not feeling well; ◆ upset etc?	
15. Do you give your child a choice of activities, outings, food etc.?	

Emotional and Behavioural Development

16. Who does your child get on with in the family?	
17. Has your child got any friends? How do they mix with them or do they play alone?	
18. How does your child settle at night and wake up in the morning? *Look at routine i.e. mealtime, food and where the child is sleeping.*	
19. Is your child talking and responding to you when you talk and play with them? If not, clarify whether the child has: ◆ special needs; ◆ hearing difficulties; ◆ sight problems; ◆ learning disabilities; ◆ other illness? *Professionals need to think about the importance of the health visitor being involved at this stage in the baby's developmental needs.*	

Getting to Know Children and Their Families, Parmar and Spatcher (2005) Russell House Publishing

Identity

20. Does your child know their own name?	
21. Is your child happy and contented or are they clingy and cry a lot?	
22. Does your child speak more than one language?	
23. How does your child communicate? *This will depend on if the child has special needs, uses Braille, or other forms of communication apart from speech.*	

Family and Social Relationships

24. Do you look after your child at home, or does someone else: ◆ at a nursery ◆ in your extended family ◆ a child minder	
25. If you have a partner which one of you takes care of your child's needs?	
26. Who is your child more attached to?	

27. How do your other children get on with your child?	
28. Do you attend a mother and toddler group?	

29. Do you take your child:
 	
  ◆ swimming;
 	
  ◆ shopping;
 	
  ◆ to meet other parents;
 	
  ◆ to participate in any other activities?
 	
Is this as a family event?	

30. Do you have any pets? If so how is your child protected from them?	
31. How does your child respond to strangers?	

Social Presentation

Observe whether the child is well cared for i.e. is it clean (no smells) well clothed and without any visible bruises. There could be 'family in need' or child protection issues.

Self-care Skills

32. Has your child started to:
 	
  ◆ dress themselves
 	
  ◆ feed themselves
 	
  ◆ wash their own hands etc.
 	
This will depend on age and ability.	

Parenting Capacity

Basic Care

33. What is the daily routine, firstly during weekdays and then weekends? ◆ what time does the child go to bed and wake up ◆ when do they have a bath ◆ when are they allowed to play ◆ what are their meal times	
34. What food does your child like to eat and what is provided for: ◆ breakfast ◆ lunch ◆ dinner ◆ snacks	
35. Is food prepared by parent or carer alone or is the child allowed to help?	
36. Does your child have adequate clothing appropriate to the weather and their age?	
37. Do you get your child seen by a GP when necessary?	
38. Does your child have their eyes and teeth checked regularly? *Take account of cultural diversity or special needs of the child or parent.*	

Ensuring Safety

39. Do you think there is adequate safety: ◆ in the kitchen ◆ on the stairs ◆ with access to the front and back doors and the garden?	
40. Is the child left with other adults apart from parents or carers, such as: ◆ extended family ◆ neighbours ◆ friends	
41. How would you safeguard your child when they are on playground equipment, out shopping, crossing roads, and going to school?	
42. Do you take your child to school? If not, why not?	

Emotional Warmth

Observe the interaction of parent or carer with the child, for example, is the child distressed and clinging or happy and content?

43. How do you comfort your child when they are upset or crying?	
44. Do you talk to your child? How (praise or rejection)?	

Getting to Know Children and Their Families, Parmar and Spatcher (2005) Russell House Publishing

Stimulation

45. Do you encourage your child to explore new experiences, such as: ◆ going to the park ◆ reading/together ◆ watching TV ◆ playing with your other children or friends?	
46. Do you go out regularly as a family? If so, where?	

Guidance and Boundaries

47. What is your child's routine: ◆ sleeping ◆ feeding ◆ playing ◆ bathing?	
48. Is your child encouraged to look after themselves by: ◆ brushing their own teeth ◆ washing themselves ◆ feeding themselves ◆ dressing themselves?	

Stability

49. Have you always cared for your child? If not, why not? (one for all).	

50. Do you have contact with family members or significant others? If not, why not?	
51. How would you describe your relationship with your child? *Explore with the parents the consistency of the close bond between them and their child.*	

Issues Affecting Parents or Carers

52. Do you have physical disabilities or mental health needs? If yes, how does this affect the care of your children?	
53. Have you had contact with social services before as an adult or a child or with your own children? If yes, when, how and why?	
54. Have you been in a relationship involving domestic violence in the past? Are you now?	
55. Have you had a problem with drink or substance misuse in the past? Do you still?	

Getting to Know Children and Their Families, Parmar and Spatcher (2005) Russell House Publishing

Family and Environmental Factors

Family History

56. What is your ethnic origin? What is your partner's ethnic origin?	
57. What was your childhood like?	
58. Did you live: ◆ with your parents ◆ in an extended family ◆ in care ◆ in this country ◆ abroad	
59. Is English your first language? If not, what is it?	
60. Do both the adults and the children in your family speak English?	

Family Functioning

61. Apart from you and your children who else lives in the house? How are they related to you and your children?	

62. Have there been any changes in the household recently, such as: ◆ a parent leaving ◆ an older child leaving home ◆ members of your extended family coming to stay ◆ a child going to live with your extended family?	
63. How do your children get on together? Do some of them get on better together than others? If so, why?	
64. If you do not live with your child's birth parent, how do you get on with them?	
65. How much contact do they have with the children? *If the birth parent that does not live in the household is different for different children, ask about each one.*	
66. If your child has special needs, what impact does this have on you and your other children?	
67. How do you handle rows, disputes, and differences of opinion in the care of your children with your partner or extended family?	

Getting to Know Children and Their Families, Parmar and Spatcher (2005) Russell House Publishing

Wider Family

68. Who from your extended family supports you with: 　◆ practical help 　◆ emotional support 　◆ financial support 　◆ interpreting 　◆ special needs help?	

Housing

69. Where do you live: 　◆ In a council house 　◆ In your own property 　◆ In B&B accommodation?	
70. How many bedrooms are there?	
71. Have all the children a bed of their own? If not, why not?	
72. Are there sufficient heating, lighting, cooking, toilet and bath facilities for the family? If not, why not?	
73. Is the home overcrowded? *Observe the hygiene, cleanliness and basic care adults are giving to the children for their emotional, and physical well-being.*	

Employment and Income

74. Are you or your partner working? If not, why not?	
75. What benefits do you receive? ◆ child benefit ◆ housing benefit ◆ (is the child support agency involved) ◆ job seekers allowance ◆ income support ◆ disability living allowance ◆ family tax credit.	
76. Do you receive money from an ex-husband or ex-partner?	
77. If you are working, are you aware of the financial support you can get?	
78. Are you managing on the money or are you in debt? *If they are not managing, suggest that they contact their local citizens advice bureau.*	
79. Does your child receive any pocket money?	

80. Does your child have school dinners, and do you pay for these?	
81. Do you budget for your bills: ◆ gas and electricity ◆ rent ◆ council tax ◆ TV licence ◆ food and school dinners ◆ clothes ◆ debts, loans ◆ bus fares?	

Family Social Integration

82. Do you have friends in the area? If not, do you feel isolated? Is this due to language and cultural problems?	
83. Do you practice a religion? Do you attend a mosque, a temple, a church etc.?	
84. Do you feel or experience discrimination or harassment in the community in which you live?	

Community Resources

85. Do you travel by public transport to access these? If so how far is it from your home?	
86. How easy is it for you to take your family on a bus or train? *This would depend on whether they have other small children as well, or a child with special needs.*	
87. Do you use the local community resources in the area: ◆ shops and supermarket ◆ library ◆ leisure activities ◆ GP/health visitor/school nurse ◆ school?	
88. Are all the family needs for leisure activities met in your local area? (Including special needs provision and children and young people's clubs). Is transport provided for them?	

Questions for Children Between 5 and 9 Years Old

The Child's Developmental Needs

Health

1. Do you have any health concerns regarding your child? What are they? Are you getting help with these?	
2. How often do you take your child to the GP/hospital? Why?	
3. Does your child go to the dentist regularly?	
4. Does your child wear glasses?	

Education

5. Is your child in full-time schooling?	
6. Does your child like school? If not why not – bullying etc?	

Getting to Know Children and Their Families, Parmar and Spatcher (2005) Russell House Publishing

7. Does your child go to school alone, with you, or with your other children?	
8. Are you happy with the school?	
9. Does your child have friends at school?	
10. Does your child get on with their teachers?	
11. Do you attend parent's evenings or other meetings at school about your child?	
12. Does your child have school lunch?	
13. Does your child have homework? Do you help them with it?	
14. Does your child need assistance with their schoolwork or help in class? (*Applies to special needs*).	

Getting to Know Children and Their Families, Parmar and Spatcher (2005) Russell House Publishing

15. Does your child have a special educational plan? (*LAC children*).	
16. Does your child attend an 'after school club' or other activities in the community?	
17. Does your child attend assembly in school? (*Depends on religious beliefs, values and school*).	

Emotional and Behavioural Development

18. Is your child aware of their own safety when: ◆ going out with friends ◆ playing outdoors ◆ going to school ◆ out in the community?	
19. Is your child able to talk to you about how they are feeling?	
20. Are you aware if your child is harming themselves by: ◆ biting ◆ scratching ◆ cutting ◆ head banging ◆ rocking ◆ glue sniffing ◆ smoking ◆ taking drugs ◆ drinking alcohol?	

21. Is your child aware of who they are? Do they value their own things?	

Identity

22. Do you get on with your child?	
23. Has your child got a temper?	
24. Who does your child get on well with in the family?	
25. Does your child have an awareness of their own cultural and racial needs? *Depends on mixed race, family.*	
26. Does your child know their name, address, birthday?	
27. Does your child know who the members of their family are?	
28. Does your child feel good about themselves? If not, why not? Are you concerned?	

29. Is your child aware of who they are? *Self-image, self-esteem, gender, age, sexuality or disability.*	

Family and Social Relationships

30. Does your child stay over night at friend's or family homes with your permission?	
31. How does your child get on with your other children?	
32. Does your child have a best friend?	
33. How would you protect your child from: ◆ harm ◆ witnessing domestic violence ◆ witnessing adult sexual behaviour ◆ strangers?	
34. Does your child know where babies come from?	

Social Presentation

Observe whether the child is well cared for i.e. is it clean (no smells) well clothed and without any visible bruises. There could be 'family in need' or child protection issues.

Getting to Know Children and Their Families, Parmar and Spatcher (2005) Russell House Publishing

Self-care Skills

35. Has your child started to:
   ◆ dress themselves
   ◆ feed themselves
   ◆ wash their hands
Depends on age and ability.	

36. Does your child help round the house for pocket money?	
37. What happens if you are ill? *The parent or carer may be disabled or have mental health issues and the child may be the main carer.*	

Getting to Know Children and Their Families, Parmar and Spatcher (2005) Russell House Publishing

Parenting Capacity

Basic Care

38. What is the daily routine, firstly during weekdays and then weekends: ◆ what time does the child go to bed and wake up ◆ when do they have a bath ◆ when are they allowed to play ◆ what are their meal times?	
39. What food does your child like to eat and what is provided for: ◆ breakfast ◆ lunch ◆ dinner ◆ snacks?	
40. Is food prepared by parent or carer alone or is the child allowed to help?	
41. Does your child have adequate clothing appropriate to the weather and their age?	
42. Do you get your child seen by a GP when necessary?	
43. Does your child have their eyes and teeth checked regularly? *Take account of cultural diversity or special needs of the child or parent.*	

Ensuring Safety

44. Do you think there is adequate safety: ◆ in the kitchen ◆ on the stairs ◆ with access to the front and back doors and the garden?	
45. Is the child left with other adults apart from parents or carers, such as: ◆ extended family ◆ neighbours ◆ friends?	
46. How would you safeguard your child when they are on playground equipment, out shopping, crossing roads, and going to school?	
47. Do you take your child to school? If not, why not?	

Emotional Warmth

Observe the reaction of the parent, or carer, with the child, for example, is the child distressed and clinging or happy and content.

48. How do you comfort your child when they are upset or crying?	
49. Do you talk to your child? How (praise or rejection)?	

Getting to Know Children and Their Families, Parmar and Spatcher (2005) Russell House Publishing

Stimulation

50. Do you encourage your child to explore new experiences, such as: 　◆ going to the park 　◆ reading/together 　◆ watching TV 　◆ playing with your other children or friends?	
51. Do you go out regularly as a family? If so, where?	
52. Is the child allowed to play outdoors with friends, or bring friends home?	
53. Does your child attend any activities out of school? 　◆ cubs 　◆ brownies 　◆ guides 　◆ scouts 　◆ fitness 　◆ after school activities or other interest groups *If the child is not attending any activities suggest some to parent or carer. This will encourage independence and promote development needs and identity.* *Observe whether the child has access to age appropriate toys, books, computers etc.*	

Guidance and Boundaries

54. Are you working? If so who looks after your child?	
55. How long are they looked after for? If looked after by a childminder, are they registered?	
56. If your child plays outside (depending on age and ability) with friends or your other children what time do they have to come home?	
57. What do you advise your child about speaking to strangers when they are out?	
58. Do you make sure you know the adults if your child is staying overnight, or visiting someone? *This includes extended family.*	

Stability

59. Have you always cared for your child? If not, why not? (one for all).	

Getting to Know Children and Their Families, Parmar and Spatcher (2005) Russell House Publishing

60. Do you have contact with family members or significant others? If not, why not?	
61. How would you describe your relationship with your child? *Explore with the parents the consistency of the close bond between them and their child.*	

Issues Affecting Parents or Carers

62. Do you have physical disabilities or mental health needs? If yes, how does this affect the care of your children?	
63. Have you had contact with social services before as an adult or a child or with your own children? If yes, when, how and why?	
64. Have you been in a relationship involving domestic violence in the past? Are you now?	
65. Have you had a problem with drink or substance misuse in the past? Do you still?	

Getting to Know Children and Their Families, Parmar and Spatcher (2005) Russell House Publishing

Family and Environmental Factors

Family History

66. What is your ethnic origin? What is your partner's ethnic origin?	
67. What was your childhood like?	
68. Did you live: ◆ with your parents ◆ in an extended family ◆ in care ◆ in this country ◆ abroad	
69. Is English your first language? If not, what is it?	
70. Do both the adults and the children in your family speak English?	

Family Functioning

71. Apart from you and your children who else lives in the house? How are they related to you and your children?	

Getting to Know Children and Their Families, Parmar and Spatcher (2005) Russell House Publishing

72. Have there been any changes in the household recently, such as: ◆ a parent leaving ◆ an older child leaving home ◆ members of your extended family coming to stay ◆ a child going to live with your extended family?	
73. How do your children get on together? Do some of them get on better together than others? If so, why?	
74. If you do not live with your child's birth parent, how do you get on with them?	
75. How much contact do they have with the children? *If the birth parent that does not live in the household is different for different children, ask about each one.*	
76. If your child has special needs, what impact does this have on you and your other children?	
77. How do you handle rows, disputes, and differences of opinion in the care of your children with your partner or extended family?	

Wider Family

78. Who from your extended family supports you with: ◆ practical help ◆ emotional support ◆ financial support ◆ interpreting ◆ special needs help?	

Housing

79. Where do you live: ◆ In a council house ◆ In your own property ◆ In B&B accommodation?	
80. How many bedrooms are there?	
81. Have all the children a bed of their own? If not, why not?	
82. Are there sufficient heating, lighting, cooking, toilet and bath facilities for the family? If not, why not?	
83. Is the home overcrowded? *Observe the hygiene, cleanliness and basic care adults are giving to the children for their emotional, and physical well-being.*	

Getting to Know Children and Their Families, Parmar and Spatcher (2005) Russell House Publishing

Employment and Income

84. Are you or your partner working? If not, why not?	
85. What benefits do you receive? ◆ child benefit ◆ housing benefit ◆ (is the child support agency involved) ◆ job seekers allowance ◆ income support ◆ disability living allowance ◆ family tax credit.	
86. Do you receive money from an ex-husband or ex-partner?	
87. If you are working, are you aware of the financial support you can get?	
88. Are you managing on the money or are you in debt? *If they are not managing, suggest that they contact their local citizens advice bureau.*	
89. Does your child receive any pocket money?	

90. Does your child have school dinners, and do you pay for these?	
91. Do you budget for your bills: ◆ gas and electricity ◆ rent ◆ council tax ◆ TV licence ◆ food and school dinners ◆ clothes ◆ debts, loans ◆ bus fares?	

Family Social Integration

92. Do you have friends in the area? If not, do you feel isolated? Is this due to language and cultural problems?	
93. Do you practice a religion? Do you attend a mosque, a temple, a church etc.?	
94. Do you feel or experience discrimination or harassment in the community in which you live?	

Community Resources

95. Do you travel by public transport to access these? If so how far is it from your home?	
96. How easy is it for you to take your family on a bus or train? *This would depend on whether they have other small children as well, or a child with special needs.*	
97. Do you use the local community resources in the area: ◆ shops and supermarket ◆ library ◆ leisure activities ◆ GP/health visitor/school nurse ◆ school?	
98. Are all the family needs for leisure activities met in your local area? (Including special needs provision and children and young people's clubs). Is transport provided for them?	

Questions for Children Between 10 and 14 Years Old

The Child's Developmental Needs

Health

1. Do you have any health concerns regarding your child? What are they? Are you getting help with these?	
2. How often do you take your child to the GP/hospital? Why?	
3. Does your child go to the dentist regularly?	
4. Does your child wear glasses?	
5. Does your child smoke or drink?	
6. If a girl, is your child having periods yet? How does she cope?	

Getting to Know Children and Their Families, Parmar and Spatcher (2005) Russell House Publishing

7. If a girl, has your child ever been pregnant? Had a child?	

Education

8. Is your child in full-time schooling?	
9. Does your child like school? If not why not – bullying etc?	
10. Does your child go to school alone, with you, or with your other children?	
11. Are you happy with the school?	
12. Does your child have friends at school?	
13. Does your child get on with their teachers?	
14. Do you attend parent's evenings or other meetings at school about your child?	

15. Does your child have school lunch?	
16. Does your child have homework? Do you help them with it?	
17. Does your child need assistance with their schoolwork or help in class? (*Applies to special needs*).	
18. Does your child have a special educational plan? (*LAC children*).	
19. Does your child attend an 'after school club' or other activities in the community?	
20. Does your child attend assembly in school? (*Depends on religious beliefs, values and school*).	

Emotional and Behavioural Development

21. Is your child aware of their own safety when: ◆ going out with friends ◆ playing outdoors ◆ going to school ◆ out in the community?	

Getting to Know Children and Their Families, Parmar and Spatcher (2005) Russell House Publishing

22. Is your child able to talk to you about how they are feeling?	
23. Are you aware if your child is harming themselves by: ◆ biting ◆ scratching ◆ cutting ◆ head banging ◆ rocking ◆ glue sniffing ◆ smoking ◆ taking drugs ◆ drinking alcohol?	
24. Is your child aware of who they are? Do they value their own things?	
25. Is your child being bullied? Do they bully others? i.e. brothers or sisters, friends, peer group.	
26. Is your child involved in drug taking, smoking?	
27. Does your child stay out late without permission?	

28. Has your child ever run away?	
29. How does your child cope when you say no to them? *Anger, frustration.*	
30. Is your child sexually active?	
31. How does your child respond to affection from you? Vice versa? *May depend on culture, sexuality, gender, disability.*	
32. Is your child happy at home?	

Identity

33. Do you get on with your child?	
34. Has your child got a temper?	
35. Who does your child get on well with in the family?	

Getting to Know Children and Their Families, Parmar and Spatcher (2005) Russell House Publishing

36. Does your child have an awareness of their own cultural and racial needs? *Depends on mixed race, family.*	
37. Does your child know their name, address, birthday?	
38. Does your child know who the members of their family are?	
39. Does your child feel good about themselves? If not, why not? Are you concerned?	
40. Is your child aware of who they are? *Self-image, self-esteem, gender, age, sexuality or disability.*	
41. When your child is in trouble, do they blame someone else?	
42. Do you value your child as a person in their own right? (*As your son or daughter and member of the family.*)	

43. Do you respect the right for your child to have different views to yours about friends, music, dress, and activities? Does your child respect yours?	

Family and Social Relationships

44. Does your child stay over night at friend's or family homes with your permission?	
45. How does your child get on with your other children?	
46. Does your child have a best friend?	
47. How would you protect your child from: ◆ harm ◆ witnessing domestic violence ◆ witnessing adult sexual behaviour ◆ strangers?	
48. Does your child know where babies come from?	

Social Presentation

Observe whether the child is well cared for i.e. is it clean (no smells) well clothed and without any visible bruises. There could be 'family in need' or child protection issues.

Getting to Know Children and Their Families, Parmar and Spatcher (2005) Russell House Publishing

Self-care Skills

49. Has your child started to:
 	
    ◆ dress themselves
 	
    ◆ feed themselves
 	
    ◆ wash their hands
 	
Depends on age and ability.	

50. Does your child help round the house for pocket money?	
51. What happens if you are ill? *The parent or carer may be disabled or have mental health issues and the child may be the main carer.*	

Parenting Capacity

Basic Care

52. What is the daily routine, firstly during weekdays and then weekends?
 	
  ◆ what time does the child go to bed and wake up
 	
  ◆ when do they have a bath
 	
  ◆ when are they allowed to play
 	
  ◆ what are their meal times	

53. What food does your child like to eat and what is provided for:
 	
  ◆ breakfast
 	
  ◆ lunch
 	
  ◆ dinner
 	
  ◆ snacks	

54. Is food prepared by parent or carer alone or is the child allowed to help?	
55. Does your child have adequate clothing appropriate to the weather and their age?	
56. Do you get your child seen by a GP when necessary?	
57. Does your child have their eyes and teeth checked regularly? *Take account of cultural diversity or special needs of the child or parent.*	

Getting to Know Children and Their Families, Parmar and Spatcher (2005) Russell House Publishing

58. Have you spoken to your child about puberty, sex and contraception? If not, why not?	
59. Does your child drink or smoke? Are there any problems with substance misuse?	
60. Does your child like school? If not, why not?	
61. Does your child have friends?	
62. Do you encourage your child to bring their friends home?	
63. Where does your child sleep? Do they share rooms with brothers or sisters?	
64. How do you discipline your child? (*Also, speak to the child about how they are disciplined.*)	

65. Is your child usually fit and healthy? If not, why not? *When visiting, check that the home is clean and adequately furnished. Observe young person for any unexplained injuries (burns, needle marks).*	

Ensuring Safety

66. Does your child let you know where they are?	
67. Do they tell you if they are going to be late home? If not, why not?	
68. Do you encourage your child to share their concerns with you about: ◆ health issues ◆ sexuality ◆ educational problems ◆ any other issues worrying them	
69. Do you provide adequate support for learning in a safe environment in the home or elsewhere?	

Emotional Warmth

70. How do you show your child that you love and care for them unconditionally?	

Getting to Know Children and Their Families, Parmar and Spatcher (2005) Russell House Publishing

71. Are you there when your child comes in from school? If not, why not?	
72. Is your child a victim of discrimination on the basis of race, religion, gender, sexuality, or disability?	
73. If yes, how do you respond in supporting your child? *Observe the physical contact and interaction between parent and child in:* ◆ *eye contact* ◆ *body language* ◆ *praise or not* ◆ *conversation*	

Stimulation

74. Do you encourage your child to explore new experiences, such as: ◆ going to the park ◆ reading/together ◆ watching TV ◆ playing with your other children or friends?	
75. Do you go out regularly as a family? If so, where?	
76. Is your child allowed to play outdoors with friends, or bring friends home?	

77. Does your child attend any activities out of school?
 	
    ◆ clubs
 	
    ◆ guides
 	
    ◆ scouts
 	
    ◆ fitness
 	
    ◆ after school activities
 	
If the child is not attending any activities suggest some to the parent or carer. This will encourage independence, promote development needs and identity.	

78. Does your child have access to appropriate education activities? e.g. computers, books.	
79. Does your child mix with their peer group outside of school? Do you encourage this? If not why not?	

Guidance and boundaries

80. Is your child allowed to attend sex education lessons at school? If not, why not?	
81. Do you talk to your child about sex education?	

Getting to Know Children and Their Families, Parmar and Spatcher (2005) Russell House Publishing

82. Do you drink, smoke, or take drugs? If yes, is this in front of your child?	

83. Do you argue with your partner in front
    of your children?
    If yes, is this physical, verbal, or both?	

84. If you do, can you think of how
    differently you can sort out your
    conflicts and problems with your
    partner?	

85. How do you deal with conflicts of
    opinion or disagreements with your
    partner concerning your child?	

86. Do you support each other in
    disciplining your child?
    If not, why not?	

87. How do you discipline your child:
 	
    ◆ visits to friends and family
 	
    ◆ time to come in
 	
    ◆ language and cultural issues	

88. If your child plays outside with friends or
    your other children, at what time do
    they have to come home?	

89. What do the parents advise the child about speaking to strangers when they are out.	
90. Do the parents make sure they know the adults, if their child is staying overnight or visiting someone? *This includes extended family.*	

Stability

91. Have you always cared for your child? If not, why not? (one for all).	
92. Do you have contact with family members or significant others? If not, why not?	
93. How would you describe your relationship with your child? *Explore with the parents the consistency of the close bond between them and their child.*	

Issues Affecting Parents or Carers

94. Do you have physical disabilities or mental health needs? If yes, how does this affect the care of your children?	

95. Have you had contact with social services before as an adult or a child or with your own children? If yes, when, how and why?	
96. Have you been in a relationship involving domestic violence in the past? Are you now?	
97. Have you had a problem with drink or substance misuse in the past? Do you still?	

Family and Environmental Factors

Family History

98. What is your ethnic origin? What is your partner's ethnic origin?	
99. What was your childhood like?	

100. Did you live:
 	
    ◆ with your parents
 	
    ◆ in an extended family
 	
    ◆ in care
 	
    ◆ in this country
 	
    ◆ abroad	

101. Is English your first language? If not, what is it?	
102. Do both the adults and the children in your family speak English?	

Family Functioning

103. Apart from you and your children who else lives in the house? How are they related to you and your children?	

Getting to Know Children and Their Families, Parmar and Spatcher (2005) Russell House Publishing

104. Have there been any changes in the household recently, such as:
 	
   ◆ a parent leaving
 	
   ◆ an older child leaving home
 	
   ◆ members of your extended family coming to stay
 	
   ◆ a child going to live with your extended family?	

105. How do your children get on together? Do some of them get on better together than others? If so, why?	
106. If you do not live with your child's birth parent, how do you get on with them?	
107. How much contact do they have with the children? *If the birth parent that does not live in the household is different for different children, ask about each one.*	
108. If your child has special needs, what impact does this have on you and your other children?	
109. How do you handle rows, disputes, and differences of opinion in the care of your children with your partner or extended family?	

Wider Family

110. Who from your extended family supports you with: ◆ practical help ◆ emotional support ◆ financial support ◆ interpreting ◆ special needs help?	

Housing

111. Where do you live: ◆ In a council house ◆ In your own property ◆ In B&B accommodation?	
112. How many bedrooms are there?	
113. Have all the children a bed of their own? If not, why not?	
114. Are there sufficient heating, lighting, cooking, toilet and bath facilities for the family? If not, why not?	

Getting to Know Children and Their Families, Parmar and Spatcher (2005) Russell House Publishing

115. Is the home overcrowded? *Observe the hygiene, cleanliness and basic care adults are giving to the children for their emotional and physical well-being.*	

Employment and Income

116. Are you or your partner working? If not, why not?	
117. What benefits do you receive? ◆ child benefit ◆ housing benefit ◆ (is the child support agency involved) ◆ job seekers allowance ◆ income support ◆ disability living allowance ◆ family tax credit.	
118. Do you receive money from an ex-husband or ex-partner?	
119. If you are working, are you aware of the financial support you can get?	
120. Are you managing on the money or are you in debt? *If they are not managing, suggest that they contact their local citizens advice bureau.*	

121. Does your child receive any pocket money?	
122. Does your child have school dinners, and do you pay for these?	
123. Do you budget for your bills: ◆ gas and electricity ◆ rent ◆ council tax ◆ TV licence ◆ food and school dinners ◆ clothes ◆ debts, loans ◆ bus fares?	

Family Social Integration

124. Do you have friends in the area? If not, do you feel isolated? Is this due to language and cultural problems?	
125. Do you practice a religion? Do you attend a mosque, a temple, a church etc.?	
126. Do you feel or experience discrimination or harassment in the community in which you live?	

Getting to Know Children and Their Families, Parmar and Spatcher (2005) Russell House Publishing

Community Resources

127. Do you travel by public transport to access these? If so how far is it from your home?	
128. How easy is it for you to take your family on a bus or train? *This would depend on whether they have other small children as well, or a child with special needs.*	
129. Do you use the local community resources in the area: ◆ shops and supermarket ◆ library ◆ leisure activities ◆ GP/health visitor/school nurse ◆ school?	
130. Are all the family needs for leisure activities met in your local area? (Including special needs provision and children and young people's clubs). Is transport provided for them?	

Getting to Know Children and Their Families, Parmar and Spatcher (2005) Russell House Publishing

Questions for Children Over 15 Years Old

The Child's Developmental Needs

Health

1. Do you have any health concerns regarding your child? What are they? Are you getting help with these?	
2. How often do you take your child to the GP/hospital? Why?	
3. Does your child go to the dentist regularly?	
4. Does your child wear glasses?	
5. Does your child smoke or drink?	
6. If a girl, is your child having periods yet? How does she cope?	

Getting to Know Children and Their Families, Parmar and Spatcher (2005) Russell House Publishing

7. If a girl, has your child ever been pregnant? Had a child?	

Education

8. Is your child in full-time schooling?	
9. Does your child like school? If not why not – bullying etc?	
10. Does your child go to school alone, with you, or with your other children?	
11. Are you happy with the school?	
12. Does your child have friends at school?	
13. Does your child get on with their teachers?	
14. Do you attend parent's evenings or other meetings at school about your child?	

15. Does your child have school lunch?	
16. Does your child have homework? Do you help them with it?	
17. Does your child need assistance with their schoolwork or help in class? *(Depends on ability of child).*	
18. Does your child have a special educational plan? *(Looked after children).*	
19. Does your child attend an 'after school club' or other activities in the community?	
20. Does your child attend assembly in school? *(Depends on religious beliefs, values and school).*	

Emotional and Behavioural Development

21. Is your child aware of their own safety when: ◆ going out with friends ◆ playing out ◆ going to school ◆ out in the community?	

Getting to Know Children and Their Families, Parmar and Spatcher (2005) Russell House Publishing

22. Is your child able to talk to you about how they are feeling?	
23. Are you aware if your child is harming themselves by: ◆ biting ◆ scratching ◆ cutting ◆ head banging ◆ rocking ◆ glue sniffing ◆ smoking ◆ taking drugs ◆ drinking alcohol?	
24. Is your child aware of who they are? Do they value their own things?	
25. Is your child being bullied? Do they bully others? i.e. brothers or sisters, friends, peer group.	
26. Is your child involved in drug taking, smoking?	
27. Does your child stay out late without permission?	

Getting to Know Children and Their Families, Parmar and Spatcher (2005) Russell House Publishing

28. Has your child ever run away?	
29. How does your child cope when you say no to them? *Anger, frustration.*	
30. Is your child sexually active?	
31. How does your child respond to affection from you? Vice versa? *May depend on culture, sexuality, gender, disability.*	
32. Is your child happy at home?	

Identity

33. Do you get on with your child?	
34. Has your child got a temper?	
35. Who does your child get on well with in the family?	

36. Does your child have an awareness of their own cultural and racial needs? *(Depends on mixed race, family and environment).*	
37. Does your child know their name, address, birthday? *(Depends on abilities).*	
38. Does your child know who the members of their family are?	
39. Does your child feel good about themselves? If not, why not? Are you concerned?	
40. Is your child aware of who they are? *(Self-image, self-esteem, gender, age, sexuality or disability).*	
41. When your child is in trouble, do they blame someone else?	
42. Do you value your child as a person in their own right? *(As your son or daughter and member of the family).*	

43. Do you respect the right for your child to have different views to yours about friends, music, dress, and activities? Does your child respect yours?	

Family and Social Relationships

44. Does your child stay over night at friend's or family homes with your permission?	
45. How does your child get on with your other children?	
46. Does your child have a best friend?	
47. How would you protect your child from: ◆ harm ◆ witnessing domestic violence ◆ witnessing adult sexual behaviour ◆ strangers?	

Social Presentation

Observe whether the child is well cared for i.e. is it clean (no smells) well clothed and without any visible bruises. There could be 'family in need' or child protection issues.

Getting to Know Children and Their Families, Parmar and Spatcher (2005) Russell House Publishing

Self-care Skills

48. Has your child started to: ◆ dress themselves ◆ feed themselves ◆ wash their hands *Depends on ability.*	
49. Does your child help round the house for pocket money?	
50. What happens if you are ill? *The parent or carer may be disabled or have mental health issues and the child may be the main carer.*	

Parenting Capacity

Basic Care

51. What is the daily routine, firstly during weekdays and then weekends? 　◆ what time does the child go to bed and wake up 　◆ when do they have a bath 　◆ when are they allowed to play 　◆ what are their meal times	
52. What food does your child like to eat and what is provided for: 　◆ breakfast 　◆ lunch 　◆ dinner 　◆ snacks	
53. Is food prepared by parent or carer alone or is the child allowed to help?	
54. Does your child have adequate clothing appropriate to the weather and their age?	
55. Do you get your child seen by a GP when necessary?	
56. Does your child have their eyes and teeth checked regularly? *Take account of cultural diversity or special needs of the child or parent.*	

57. Have you spoken to your child about puberty, sex and contraception? If not, why not?	
58. Does your child drink or smoke? Are there any problems with substance misuse?	
59. Does your child like school? If not, why not?	
60. Does your child have friends?	
61. Do you encourage your child to bring their friends home?	
62. Where does your child sleep? Do they share rooms with brothers or sisters?	
63. How do you discipline your child? *(Also, speak to the child about how they are disciplined).*	

Getting to Know Children and Their Families, Parmar and Spatcher (2005) Russell House Publishing

| 64. Is your child usually fit and healthy? If not, why not? *When visiting, check that the home is clean and adequately furnished. Observe young person for any unexplained injuries (burns, needle marks).* | |

Ensuring Safety

65. Does your child let you know where they are?	
66. Does your child tell you if they are going to be late home? If not, why not?	
67. Do you encourage your child to share their concerns with you over: ◆ health issues ◆ sexuality ◆ educational problems ◆ any other issues worrying them?	
68. Do you provide adequate support for learning in a safe environment in the home or elsewhere?	

Emotional Warmth

| 69. How do you show your child that you love and care for them unconditionally? | |

Getting to Know Children and Their Families, Parmar and Spatcher (2005) Russell House Publishing

70. Are you there when your child comes in from school? If not, why not?	
71. Is your child a victim of discrimination on the basis of race, religion, gender, sexuality, or disability?	
72. If yes, how do you respond in supporting your child? *Observe the physical contact and interaction between parent and child in:* ◆ *eye contact* ◆ *body language* ◆ *praise or not* ◆ *conversation*	

Stimulation

73. Do you encourage your child to explore new experiences, such as: ◆ going to the park ◆ reading/together ◆ watching TV ◆ playing with your other children or friends?	
74. Do you go out regularly as a family? If so, where?	
75. Is the child allowed to play outdoors with friends, or bring friends home?	

76. Does your child attend any activities out of school?
 	
    ◆ clubs
 	
    ◆ guides
 	
    ◆ scouts
 	
    ◆ fitness
 	
    ◆ after school activities
 	
If they are not attending any activities, suggest to the parents that this might encourage independence, promote development needs and identity.	

77. Does your child have access to age appropriate educational facilities? e.g. computers, books.	
78. Does your child mix with their peer group outside of school? Do you encourage this? If not, why not?	

Guidance and boundaries

79. Is your child allowed to attend sex education lessons at school? If not, why not?	
80. Do you talk to your child about sex education?	

81. Do you drink, smoke, or take drugs? If yes, is this in front of your child?	
82. Do you argue with your partner in front of your children? If yes, is this physical, verbal, or both?	
83. If you do, can you think of how differently you can sort out your conflicts and problems with your partner?	
84. How do you deal with conflicts of opinion or disagreements with your partner concerning your child?	
85. Do you support each other in disciplining your child? If not, why not?	
86. How do you discipline your child: ◆ visits to friends and family ◆ time to come in ◆ language and cultural issues	
87. If your child plays outside with friends or your other children, at what time do they have to come home?	

88. What do the parents advise the child about speaking to strangers when they are out.	
89. Do the parents make sure they know the adults, if their child is staying overnight or visiting someone? *This includes extended family.*	

Stability

90. Have you always cared for your child? If not, why not? (one for all).	
91. Do you have contact with family members or significant others? If not, why not?	
92. How would you describe your relationship with your child? *Explore with the parents the consistency of the close bond between them and their child.*	

Issues Affecting Parents or Carers

93. Do you have physical disabilities or mental health needs? If yes, how does this affect the care of your children?	

94. Have you had contact with social services before as an adult or a child or with your own children? If yes, when, how and why?	
95. Have you been in a relationship involving domestic violence in the past? Are you now?	
96. Have you had a problem with drink or substance misuse in the past? Do you still?	

Family and Environmental Factors

Family History

97. What is your ethnic origin? What is your partner's ethnic origin?	
98. What was your childhood like?	
99. Did you live: ◆ with your parents ◆ in an extended family ◆ in care ◆ in this country ◆ abroad	
100. Is English your first language? If not, what is it?	
101. Do both the adults and the children in your family speak English?	

Family Functioning

102. Apart from you and your children who else lives in the house? How are they related to you and your children?	

Getting to Know Children and Their Families, Parmar and Spatcher (2005) Russell House Publishing

103. Have there been any changes in the household recently, such as: ◆ a parent leaving ◆ an older child leaving home ◆ members of your extended family coming to stay ◆ a child going to live with your extended family?	
104. How do your children get on together? Do some of them get on better together than others? If so, why?	
105. If you do not live with your child's birth parent, how do you get on with them?	
106. How much contact do they have with the children? *If the birth parent that does not live in the household is different for different children, ask about each one.*	
107. If your child has special needs, what impact does this have on you and your other children?	
108. How do you handle rows, disputes, and differences of opinion in the care of your children with your partner or extended family?	

Wider Family

109. Who from your extended family supports you with:
 	
    ◆ practical help
 	
    ◆ emotional support
 	
    ◆ financial support
 	
    ◆ interpreting
 	
    ◆ special needs help?	

Housing

110. Where do you live:
 	
    ◆ In a council house
 	
    ◆ In your own property
 	
    ◆ In B&B accommodation?	

111. How many bedrooms are there?	
112. Have all the children a bed of their own? If not, why not?	
113. Are there sufficient heating, lighting, cooking, toilet and bath facilities for the family? If not, why not?	
114. Is the home overcrowded? *Observe the hygiene, cleanliness and basic care adults are giving to the children for their emotional, and physical well-being.*	

Employment and Income

115. Are you or your partner working? If not, why not?	
116. What benefits do you receive? ◆ child benefit ◆ housing benefit ◆ (is the child support agency involved) ◆ job seekers allowance ◆ income support ◆ disability living allowance ◆ family tax credit.	
117. Do you receive money from an ex-husband or ex-partner?	
118. If you are working, are you aware of the financial support you can get?	
119. Are you managing on the money or are you in debt? *If they are not managing, suggest that they contact their local citizens advice bureau.*	
120. Does your child receive any pocket money?	

121. Does your child have school dinners, and do you pay for these?	
122. Do you budget for your bills: ◆ gas and electricity ◆ rent ◆ council tax ◆ TV licence ◆ food and school dinners ◆ clothes ◆ debts, loans ◆ bus fares?	

Family Social Integration

123. Do you have friends in the area? If not, do you feel isolated? Is this due to language and cultural problems?	
124. Do you practice a religion? Do you attend a mosque, a temple, a church etc.?	
125. Do you feel or experience discrimination or harassment in the community in which you live?	

Community Resources

126. Do you travel by public transport to access these? If so how far is it from your home?	
127. How easy is it for you to take your family on a bus or train? *This would depend on whether they have other small children as well, or a child with special needs.*	
128. Do you use the local community resources in the area: ◆ shops and supermarket ◆ library ◆ leisure activities ◆ GP/health visitor/school nurse ◆ school?	
129. Are all the family needs for leisure activities met in your local area? (Including special needs provision and children and young people's clubs). Is transport provided for them?	

References

Calder, M.C. and Hackett, S. (Eds.) (2003) *Assessment in Child Care: Using and Developing Frameworks for Practice.* Lyme Regis: Russell House Publishing.

Calder, M.C. et al. (2000) *The Complete Guide to Sexual Abuse Assessments.* Lyme Regis: Russell House Publishing.

Cox, A. and Bentovin, A. (2000) *The Family Assessment Pack of Questionnaires and Scales.* London: The Stationery Office.

Department of Health (1999) *Working Together to Safeguard Children, A Guide to Inter-agency Working to Safeguard and Promote the Welfare of Children.* London: The Stationery Office.

Department of Health (2000) *Framework for Assessment for Children in Need and their Families.* London: The Stationery Office.

Department of Health (2001) *The Children Act Now, Messages from Research.* London: The Stationery Office.

Reder, P., Duncan, S. and Gray, M. (2002) *Beyond Blame, Child Abuse Tragedies Revisited.* London: Routledge.

White, R., Carr, A.P. and Lowe, N. (1991) *A Guide to the Children Act 1989.* London: Butterworths.

Reading List

Adock, M. (2000) *The Core Assessment: How to Synthesise Information and Make Judgements.* In Horwath, J. (Ed.) (2000) *The Child's World, Assessing Children in Need. The Reader.* London: NSPPC.

Cleaver, H., Unell, I. and Aldgate, J. (1999) *Children's Needs – Parenting Capacity; The Impact of Parental Mental Illness, Problem Alcohol and Drug Use, and Domestic Violence on Children's Development.* London: The Stationery Office.

Department of Health (1989) *An Introduction to the Children Act 1989.* London: HMSO.

Department of Health (1991) *The Children Act (1989) Guidance and Regulations. Vol 1–10.* London: HMSO.

Department of Health (2000b) *Assessing Children in Need and their Families; Practice Guidance.* London: The Stationery Office.

Department of Health (2000c) *Studies Which Inform the Development of the Framework for the Assessment of Children in Need and their Families.* London: The Stationery Office.